Reel It In

BASS FISHING

Tina P. Schwartz

PowerKiDS press.

New York

To Lorijo Metz—Thanks for your constant support,
and for the intro to Amelie at Rosen! With love, Tina P.

Published in 2012 by The Rosen Publishing Group, Inc.
29 East 21st Street, New York, NY 10010

First Edition

Editor: Amelie von Zumbusch
Book Design: Kate Laczynski

Photo Credits: Cover © www.iStockphoto.com/Midwest Wilderness; pp. 4, 11 (top), 13, 14, 17 (top), 19 Shutterstock.com; pp. 5, 6, 17 (bottom), 18, 22 iStockphoto/Thinkstock; p. 7 Gary Meszaros/Getty Images; pp. 8–9 © www.iStockphoto.com/George Peters; p. 10 © www.iStockphoto.com/Dave Willman; p. 11 (bottom) © www.iStockphoto.com/Michael Olson; p. 12 © age fotostock/SuperStock; p. 15 © www.iStockphoto.com/Daniel Gangur; p. 16 Sam Diephuis/Getty Images; p. 20 Bob Rosato/Sports Illustrated/Getty Images; p. 21 KMazur/WireImage/Getty Images.

Library of Congress Cataloging-in-Publication Data

Schwartz, Tina P., 1969–
  Bass fishing / by Tina P. Schwartz. — 1st ed.
      p. cm. — (Reel it in)
  Includes index.
  ISBN 978-1-4488-6201-6 (library binding) — ISBN 978-1-4488-6361-7 (pbk.) —
  ISBN 978-1-4488-6362-4 (6-pack)
  1. Bass fishing—Juvenile literature. I. Title.
  SH681.S35 2012
  799.17'73—dc23
                                        2011034837

Manufactured in the United States of America

CPSIA Compliance Information: Batch #WW12PK: For Further Information contact Rosen Publishing, New York, New York at 1-800-237-9932

CONTENTS

Bass Fishing Is Fun!

Why is bass fishing so great? For one thing, there are several types of bass in North America. These fish are also fairly easy to find. They live in many places, such as creeks, streams, rivers, lakes, **reservoirs**, and ponds. Bass tend to fight back after they are hooked. This makes them exciting to catch.

Many people catch bass in lakes, as this boy has done.

This girl caught a bass. Bass are members of the sunfish family.

The sport has become so popular that you can find bass-fishing **tournaments** all over the United States.

Anglers, or fishermen, of all ages can participate in bass fishing. You can even watch TV shows about bass fishing. On these shows, master fishermen share their fishing tips.

The three main **species**, or kinds, of bass are largemouth bass, smallmouth bass, and spotted bass. Largemouth bass like calm waters best but also live in other kinds of water. They are olive green.

Smallmouth bass are brownish. They often have dark lines up and down their sides. They are more

Largemouth bass, like the one this man caught, are named for their wide mouths.

commonly found in moving water, such as streams and rivers, than largemouth bass. Smallmouth bass also like rocky areas.

Spotted bass are smaller than largemouth bass but bigger than smallmouth bass. They like deep waters with rocky bottoms. Spotted bass have rows of spots along the undersides of their bodies. They often travel in groups, called **schools**.

FUN FISH FACT

Largemouth bass, smallmouth bass, and spotted bass are part of a group of fish called black bass. The Guadalupe bass, which lives only in parts of Texas, is another black bass.

This is a smallmouth bass. Smallmouth bass tend to be found in cooler waters than largemouth bass.

Where to Fish

The hardest part about bass fishing is finding where the fish are. Bass move around as the seasons change. They also move around due to the **temperature** of the water. Fish will swim to places where more food is available, too. They also move around based on how high the water is and how much light shines through it. Bass like to be near weeds, rocks, or logs. This gives them a hiding place, shade, and food.

Bass most often **spawn**, or lay their eggs, in shallow waters in late winter and early spring. This is when they are easiest to catch.

This angler caught a largemouth bass from a canoe. A boat can help you reach parts of a lake that would otherwise be too far from shore or too deep to reach.

Bait and Tackle

To fish for bass, you will need **tackle**, or gear. Most people use a rod and **reel**. The reel holds line. The end of the line often has a hook with **bait**, such as a crayfish, on it. Some anglers use man-made **lures** instead of baited hooks.

You can see part of the lure this angler used in the mouth of the largemouth bass he caught.

Some anglers use a tackle box, such as this one, to carry most of their tackle.

You might also need a fishing **license**. This is a paper that allows you to go fishing. Some states require a license, while others do not.

After you reel in your catch, it helps to have a net handy. This is the easiest way to scoop up your catch, especially if it is struggling to swim away.

This woman used a reel and rod to catch a smallmouth bass in Lake Michigan.

Casting for Bass

Some people choose to walk out into the middle of a river to cast. This can get them closer to the fish.

Most bass fishermen use one of three methods to cast their line. These are the overhand cast, sidearm cast, and underhand cast. Each name describes how you move your hand as you cast. One tip to remember when casting is to try to make the lure land on the water as quietly as you can. Also, cast with your wrist, not your shoulder or arm.

Practicing your casting is a great idea. A good place to do this is on a pond or some other **still water**. Practicing on grass is okay if there is no water around, but practicing on water is best.

Make sure that there is nobody around who could get in the way when you practice casting. People can be hurt badly if they get caught with a hook.

Fly-Fishing for Bass

Though most people use a normal rod and reel to fish for bass, some use a fly-fishing rod. Fly-fishing rods are longer and lighter than other rods. Fishing with these rods is called fly-fishing. People use special lures called flies for fly-fishing. Flies are made out of string or feathers. Many flies look a bit like real insects.

Casting a fly-fishing rod takes a lot of skill. If you have trouble at first, keep practicing. You can ask a long-time fly fisherman for tips, too.

Bass poppers, such as this one, are a kind of fly made for catching bass.

When fly-casting, you are really casting your line, not the fly. When you cast, the line flies out in the direction in which you aim the rod. This means you need to make your movements as smooth as possible.

After the Catch

You finally caught a fish. Great job! Now you have to decide if you are going to release it back into the water. If you do this, someone else can catch it another day.

You could also eat the fish you catch. After an adult cleans and guts your fish, you could ask the adult to cook it on the grill. What a delicious treat to share!

In many states, there are laws that say bass under a certain size must be released.

This is a largemouth bass trophy. Trophies are sometimes mounted on a piece of wood, as this one is.

Another possibility is to have your catch made into a **trophy,** or prize. Then you could put it on the wall for all of your friends to see. There are so many possibilities!

It is a good idea to decide what you will do with a bass you are trying to catch before you catch it.

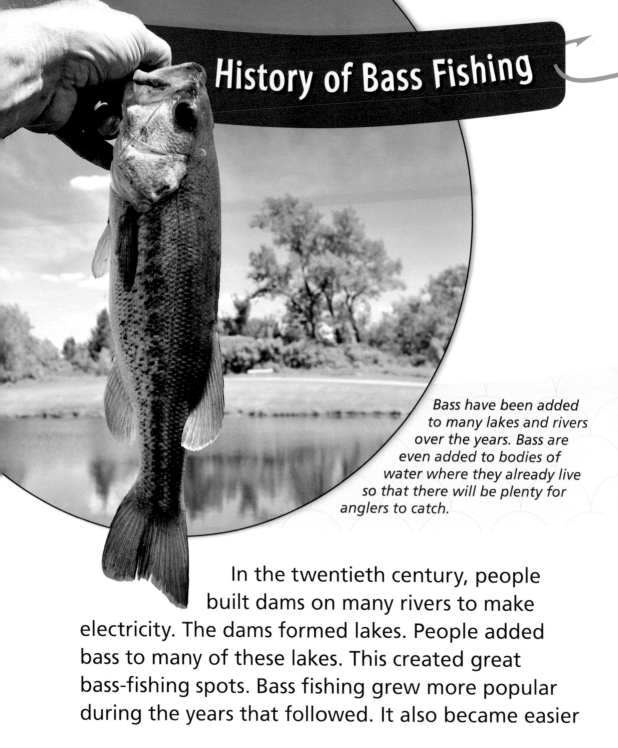

History of Bass Fishing

Bass have been added to many lakes and rivers over the years. Bass are even added to bodies of water where they already live so that there will be plenty for anglers to catch.

In the twentieth century, people built dams on many rivers to make electricity. The dams formed lakes. People added bass to many of these lakes. This created great bass-fishing spots. Bass fishing grew more popular during the years that followed. It also became easier thanks to new inventions, such as advanced fishing reels.

One famous early bass fisherman was George W. Perry. In 1932, he caught a largemouth bass in Georgia that weighed 22 pounds 4 ounces (10.1 kg). This set a record for the biggest bass ever caught. It remained unbroken for over 75 years!

Lake Powell, in Arizona and Utah, was formed when the Glen Canyon Dam was built on the Colorado River in 1963. The lake was stocked with both smallmouth bass and largemouth bass.

Bass-Fishing Tournaments

Here, bass pro Mike Iaconelli is taking part in the Bassmaster Classic. Iaconelli is a famous bass pro. He is from New Jersey.

If you love bass fishing, you might want to enter a bass-fishing tournament. In a tournament, people try to catch the biggest bass or the largest number of bass. The rules are different from one tournament to another. In some, you lose points if a fish dies. There are tournaments open only to kids or teenagers.

Bass pros make a living by taking part in the biggest tournaments. They can win a lot of money in these tournaments. For example, the winner of the Bassmaster Classic tournament gets $500,000. Tournament winners become big stars. Kevin VanDam, Rick Clunn, and Edwin Evers are some famous bass anglers.

Kevin VanDam has won many awards during his years as a bass pro. Here he is holding the 2002 ESPY Award for Best Outdoor Athlete.

The Future of Bass Fishing

When you go bass fishing, be responsible. Pick up any trash you see around your fishing spot. Do not leave extra line or hooks around. Birds or other animals could try to eat them and end up choking.

Today, bass are the kind of fish that American anglers most often aim to catch. People like bass fishing for many reasons. It lets you spend time in

Millions of Americans enjoy bass fishing. It is a great sport!

nature. It is a fun sport to do with friends and family. You can make memories that will last a lifetime!

GLOSSARY

anglers (ANG-glerz) People who fish with rods and reels.

bait (BAYT) Something that is used to draw in animals being fished or hunted.

license (LY-suns) Official permission to do something.

lures (LUHRZ) Objects used for bait.

reel (REEL) Something around which line or thread is wound.

reservoirs (REH-zuh-vwarz) Stored bodies of water.

schools (SKOOLZ) Groups of fish.

spawn (SPAWN) To come together to lay eggs.

species (SPEE-sheez) One kind of living thing. All people are one species.

still water (STIL WAH-ter) Water that is not flowing, such as that in a lake or pond.

tackle (TA-kul) The gear and tools used for fishing as a hobby.

temperature (TEM-pur-cher) How hot or cold something is.

tournaments (TOR-nuh-ments) Events to decide who is the best at something.

trophy (TROH-fee) An exact copy of a fish made to show others one's catch.

INDEX

24 Sept '13

WEB SITES

Due to the changing nature of Internet links, PowerKids Press has developed an online list of Web sites related to the subject of this book. This site is updated regularly. Please use this link to access the list:
www.powerkidslinks.com/reel/bass/